Building an Off-Grid Solar System

Mobile Off-the-Grid Solar Power for RVs, Van Life, and Boats

By

Judson Crawford

SPECIAL OFFER

Want this bonus book for free?

Get <u>FREE</u>, unlimited access to it and all of my new books by joining my Launch Club!

Table of Contents

Introduction

Every time you hear someone say they are thinking of going off-grid, the first thing that comes to mind is solar power. I mean, what could be more off-grid than getting power from the sun? For many people, living 100 percent off-grid would be a dream come true. Not only would you save money but it's great for the environment. In recent years inflation and hard economic times have caused an increase in the cost of basic utilities such as electricity. It's not hard to see why you want to go in this direction.

Until recently, going off-grid was considered as something for hardcore survivalists. You had to know how to live off the land and forget the amenities you have become so accustomed to. However, thanks to advancements in technology, living or going off-grid doesn't mean going back to the Stone Age. It has become much easier to make the transition; all you need are a few tools and some technical know-how, and you are good to go. Sounds easy, right? In essence, it is; however it still requires you to have some technical skill. That's where I come in. Having lived seven years on the road, I have learned quite a lot about building an off-grid solar system.

As a mobile home owner, van dweller, RVer, or boondocker, you are no stranger to the outdoors, and you might be thinking about adding an off-grid solar system to help power your rig. Transitioning to solar power, while very easy, can be intimidating. After all, putting together a solar system isn't a fifteen-minute job. It takes time but don't let the technicality of the work put you off. There are benefits to solar power, such as its affordability. The cost of solar system components, including battery storage, has gone down considerably, making it a more affordable and cost-effective way to power your dwelling.

What does living off-grid really mean?

The premise behind going off-grid is pretty straightforward: just unplug from the world. This means living off the land. From a power perspective, it means unplugging yourself from the electricity grid. With an off-grid power source, you don't need to access the greater electricity grid; essentially, you create your own grid that powers your home. Going off-grid means living autonomously without relying on the main electricity grid. You live, instead, on alternative power sources such as solar power. As a utility, electricity is expected to achieve three things: generation, transmission, and distribution. This means the power station handles the generation, and the grid handles the transmission and distribution. People consider going off-grid because they want independence from the grid, to exert control over their power usage, and lower their energy costs.

If you merely want to gain an understanding of how solar power works or you are planning on installing an off-grid solar system, this book contains all the information you need. You'll learn how solar power works, how to harness it, and how to design and install your very own solar system. While having some electrical knowledge is not required, it does come in handy. This doesn't mean you can't design and install your own off-grid solar power system; it just implies it will take a lot longer for you to get it done because you have to get caught up on the fundamentals first. Let's dive in.

CHAPTER ONE

Solar Electricity: The Basics

Before we get to the design and installation part, let's go through some solar basics.

Where does Solar Energy Come From?

Solar energy comes from the sun. The radiation produced by the intense nuclear activity going on both on and under the surface generates photons or light energy. These photons contain massive amounts of solar energy, which is transmitted to the earth at different wavelengths. Some carry non-visible light such as infra-red or ultraviolet rays, while others carry visible light, often referred to as white light. Picture the sun as a giant nuclear reactor producing radiation whose power is then carried to the earth by photons.

These photons travel at incredible speeds and can reach the earth's surface in about eight minutes. Every hour, enough photons travel to the earth's surface to produce enough solar energy to theoretically satisfy the world's energy needs if harnessed at 100 percent efficiency. However, not all photons reach the earth's surface; some collide with particles in outer space and are destroyed after their radiation is absorbed. Others get absorbed by the earth's atmosphere and clouds, and only about 46 percent reach the surface. Of this, 46 percent, 50 percent is white light, 45 percent is infrared radiation, and the remaining 5 percent is UV rays and other electromagnetic radiation.

The earth's atmosphere absorbs most of the photons that reach the Earth; that's why even though the sun emits its radiation at the same intensity throughout the day, it reaches us at fluctuating strengths, depending on the time of day and the weather. For instance, at midday, the sun feels hotter because the atmosphere is saturated with photons allowing more to get to the surface. They also travel a shorter distance through thinner atmospheric layers to get to the surface. In the morning or evening, the distance between the sun and the surface is further, and the layer's thicker, so the amount of radiation that reaches the surface is greatly reduced. That's why some days, even though it's sunny, it is still cold because only white light is getting through.

What is Solar Electricity?

Solar electricity is electricity generated using the photovoltaic effect of the sun. This phenomenon occurs because certain materials such as selenium or silicon produce an electric current when exposed to sunlight. It's both a chemical and physical process that converts the sun's light energy into electrical energy. For this effect to occur, two layers of semi-conducting material, say silicon, must be combined: the p-type (positive) and the n-type (negative). When joined using a p-n junction, they establish an electric field where electrons move from the p-side and holes to the n-side.

If the silicon is then exposed to the sun, it absorbs photons that transfer energy to the electrons of the silicon. This raises their energy state, making them jump from one valence band to another, leaving a hole. Instead of flowing to the positive end, the freed electrons flow to the negative end. This movement of electrons creates electric current, and, because of the nature of the electric field existing because of the p-n junction, the electrons flow in the opposite direction.

Solar cells are made from thin layers or wafers of silicon. Some of them are doped to create a greater electron imbalance. The silicon wafers are then aligned and joined using metallic strips to create solar cells. When the silicon absorbs a photon, it produces electricity; the more photons absorbed, the more electricity you get, and vice-versa. This means that the amount of electricity produced is equivalent to the intensity of light absorbed. Individually these cells don't create that much electricity; however, when they are connected together in a solar panel, their electrical output is significantly increased.

A Bit of Solar History

Solar energy tech has come a long way; this is what has majorly contributed to the reducing cost of materials and components. Evidence of solar energy use dates back to the 7th century where humans used solar power to light fires; in the 3rd-century, Greeks and Romans pushed this further by harnessing solar power wing mirrors. From the 1700s to the 1800s, sailors often used the energy of the sun to power their steamboats. As you can see, the concept of manipulating and harnessing the sun's power started long ago.

However, the solar panel wasn't invented until much later, and various scientists contributed to its creation. In 1873, Willoughby Smith discovered the photoconductive potential of selenium, which led William Grylls Adams and Richard Evans to discover that it creates electricity when exposed to sunlight. In 1883, Charles Fritts made the first solar cells from selenium, but today's solar cells are made from silicon, not selenium. This discovery was made by Daryl Chapin and his colleagues in 1954 as they invented the first silicon-made photovoltaic (PV) cell capable of powering an electronic device for several hours.

The first silicon solar cells could only convert solar energy at 4 percent. This is the amount of solar energy converted to electricity. That's pretty low; however, thanks to advancements in tech, cells today have a conversion efficiency of about 20 percent, with some cells reaching 35 to 40 percent. In 2019, researchers at National Renewable Energy Laboratory, Golden, Colorado, set the world record by creating cells with an efficiency rating of 47 percent. This was achieved by using multi-junction concentrator solar cells. They surpassed the standard polycrystalline photovoltaic cells, which have an efficiency rating of 37 percent.

The cost of solar equipment has gradually dropped over time. In 1956 the cost of solar panels was $300/W; by 1975, it had dropped to about $100/W. Today you could pay as little as $0.50/W. This is because the price of solar panels drops by about 10 percent every year, largely in part due to the increased popularity of solar energy as a renewable power source.

Solar Electricity Expectations

While solar electricity is wonderful, it does have some limitations. For instance, the sun isn't a continuous power source; the amount of power you can generate depends on the amount of sunlight or irradiance you get, the location you are in, and whether the panel is free from shade. If you plan to use solar electricity as the only source of power, you need to ensure that you are getting enough power. You also need to keep your consumption low and rethink your consumption. Remember that this type of electricity is not well-suited for particulate tasks such as generating heat, so if you need heating, you must try using something else.

The sun provides all the energy you need to exist, from driving the climate to powering our bodies; it is undoubtedly a huge energy source. Harnessing the sun's energy means no more electricity bills, and it's good for the environment. However, the reality is a bit different.

You need to know how it all works. What is solar power suitable for? Are there any limitations? How easy is it to install? And so on. There are loads of myths surrounding solar power and going off-grid. While it is easy to see the allure of going off-grid by plugging into a renewable power source such as solar energy, actually doing it requires a bit more work than you would think. As a long-time off-gridder, I want to debunk some of the myths.

Myth 1: Going off-grid is expensive - going off-grid requires a lot of equipment. There was a time when the cost of this equipment made people shy away from adopting solar energy. Nowadays, however, thanks to advancements in technology, these components are considerably cheaper.

Myth 2: Going off-grid means a simple life - managing and maintaining your own grid takes time and skill. Remember, you are now in charge of generation, transmission, and distribution, which means that you have to work out most of the nitty-gritty stuff that's going on. For instance, failing to check for loose or corroded wires can lead to a system failure, and your batteries need some TLC every once in a while. Overall, going off the grid increases your workload.

Myth 3: You can still do things the same way you used to - going off-grid means cutting out a lot of devices that use up energy gluttonously. While solar power is renewable, if your battery runs out, you won't have any more power; you have to wait until your battery gets fully-charged again. This means that you can't use off-grid power the same way you use on-grid power. Plugging in too many appliances or devices at once will drain your battery quicker. This means you have to seriously reevaluate what you need to power.

How Much Power Can I Get?

Solar panels convert the sun's energy into electricity through the photovoltaic effect. The amount of electricity produced is measured in watt-hours (Wh). How much you get will depend on the wattage rating of the panel. For instance, a panel rated 300 watts (W) panel produces 300 watts per hour. This means that in about five hours, it would produce about 1500 watt-hours or 1.5 kilowatt-hours.

That is 5 hours x 300W = 1500Wh.

In a month, that's about 45000 Wh or 45kWh. This is enough to power small appliances around the house, but you need more or higher-capacity panels for larger appliances. Other factors that can affect a solar panel's electricity output are its size, location, and weather conditions.

To calculate how much electricity you get from your solar panel a day, use this formula:

Solar panel size in square meters x 1000.

Multiply the result by the panel's efficiency, then multiply that result by the number of sun hours. Finally, divide your final result by 1000 to get the value in kilowatt-hours.

Here's an easy example to help clear things up.

If you have a panel that measures 1.7 square meters, then multiply it by 1000:

1.7 x 1000 = 1700.

Multiply 1700 by the efficiency of the panel, which is 20 percent.

1600 x 20/100 = 340.

If you get about 5 hours of sunlight a day, then multiply 340 by 5.

340 x 5 = 1700 watt-hours.

Divide this resulting value by 1000 to get the value in kilowatt-hours.

1700/1000 = 1.7 kWh.

Photovoltaic (PV) Components

Photovoltaic systems are pretty straightforward: connect a panel to a load and use the load as you wish. Each solar system varies in capacity and design; however, despite all these differences, they contain similar components. These are:

- The PV modules or cells - these are the individual units made of PV cells that make up a PV array. They produce the electrical energy used to power your solar system.
- Battery banks - batteries offer a way to store the electricity produced by PV modules. Several

batteries connected together make up a battery bank that stores the system's power.

- Inverters - these devices convert the direct current (DC) generated by the panel into alternating current (AC). These inverters also adjust the voltage of PV cells down to the AC or grid voltage and control power output in case of instability.
- Disconnect and overcurrent protection - these components, such as circuit breakers, fuses, etc., control and limit the amount of current flowing in a system. This ensures the safety of the system and those using it. You wouldn't want your battery pack bursting into flames because of too much current.

These are just some of the essential components you will find in a PV system. We will take a deeper look at all the nitty-gritty stuff you need later on.

CHAPTER TWO

Determining Your Budget and Needs

The first step of the design process is figuring out what you need and how much everything will cost you. No matter what you are planning on using your PV system for, these simple steps will help guide you.

Step 1: Think About the Scope of the Project

Think about what you want to achieve? What is the reason behind starting the project? Here are a few examples:

- To power the lighting system.
- To power small household equipment.
- To power an RV or camper.
- To charge electric bikes between uses.

Your project's scope gives you the main idea of what you are trying to achieve. Keep things simple, so you have a better idea of what you need to do. From here, you can properly flesh it out and determine proper estimates instead of working with abstractions. For instance, start simple; say you want to build a system that powers your mobile home. Then add more detail to this by specifying what you want to power; you want to provide all the electrical power your mobile home needs including lighting, and powering small appliances. Take it a step further by specifying how long this system will run, for instance, between March and October, plus a few winter weekends. Going off-grid is an ambitious process, so make sure you get the scope right. Getting it wrong can lead to you designing and creating a system that will not meet your needs.

When going off-grid, the system you create will provide all of your power. Unlike with a grid-tie system, any miscalculations or overuse and you will be left in the dark. At this point, you need to quantify what you want to achieve and estimate some of your energy needs. Performing a power analysis can help you determine your needs and determine the size of your system. Check the labels or manuals of your devices to find out how much wattage you require. Fleshing out your scope includes comparing your supply and demand by determining your monthly power needs. For instance, think about what kinds of equipment or appliances you want to power. If you are thinking of powering your RV, aside from basic appliances, you also have to account for extra energy for charging your phone or laptop.

After determining what equipment you need to power, find out how much power and energy each device needs and estimate their daily usage. Remember, the point is to keep efficiency high and costs low so work with as many low voltage devices as you can instead of getting a high voltage grid. However, if you can't switch them out, working with an inverter to step down grid voltage is an easier option. As you come up with a rough estimate of what you need, remember that batteries are not 100 percent efficient. This means they won't return 100 percent of the energy used to charge them. A battery's charge cycle efficiency is the measure of the available energy compared to the energy used to charge it. While this figure varies, it ranges between 90 to 95 for most batteries. If you are using an inverter, don't forget to account for its inefficiencies.

Step 2: Calculate the Amount of Energy You Need

Next is figuring out how much solar energy you need. Keeping to the mobile home example, your power analysis would look something like this:

Device	Wattage	Voltage	Hours used daily	Watt-hours
Lighting	11W	12V	4	44Wh
Small fridge	12W	12V	24	288Wh
TV	40W	12V	3	120Wh
Laptop	40W	12V	1	40Wh
Phone charging	5W	12V	4	20Wh
Other loads	2W	12V	24	48Wh
Total energy consumption				560Wh

As a rule of thumb, always add about 10 percent of your total consumption to account for any system inefficiencies. For our example, your total consumption would be:

560 x 10 % = 56

560 + 56 = 616Wh

If you are not utilizing an inverter, then multiply your total consumption by 5 percent to account for the battery's charge cycle efficiency. In this case, your consumption would be:

560 x 5 % = 28

560 + 28 = 588Wh

Next is calculating solar energy.

Solar energy is the total of how much energy you get from the strength of the sun's rays and the hours of sunlight you get. Also referred to as the sun's irradiance, it is expressed in W/m2. This matters because PV cells quote the number of watts they can generate based on the solar irradiance of 1 kilowatt per square meter, denoted as watts-peak (Wp). It shows how much energy the panel can produce in ideal conditions. To calculate how much solar energy your panel will produce, first find out the solar irradiance and multiply this by your panel's wattage rating.

Keep in mind that solar irradiance varies depending on which month it is—the more cloudy the weather, the lower the irradiance. The panel's angle or tilt also plays a role in improving or decreasing the irradiance your panel receives. For instance, let's say in January, the solar irradiance is 0.8. If you mount your solar panel upright, it will increase to 1.3. At a 38 degree tilt, which is ideal for year-round performance, it would be 1. 37. If you lower it to 23 degrees instead because this position works best in winter, the solar radiance would be 1.4.

The optimal tilt varies throughout the year because the earth is on a 23.5-degree tilt. For some installations, you might need to adjust their tilt monthly. Here's a simple way to figure out your optimum tilt:

90 degrees - your latitude = optimal tilt degree setting

Determining the optimal tilt setting will help you get the most power from your system, especially in winter when the sun is scarce.

When positioning your panels, remember, no matter where you are, the sun rises and sets in the same direction. That said, if you are in the northern hemisphere, your panels will be more efficient if they are facing southward and vice-versa. If you face your panels toward the East or West, expect about a 20 percent decrease in efficiency. If you faced them north in the northern hemisphere and south in the southern hemisphere, expect a 40 percent decrease in efficiency.

PV panels and shade: Shade can make a really big impact on your project. Even if only a small part of your panel is covered by the shade, it can significantly impact the panel's output. Depending on the circumstances, even if only about 5 percent is shaded, this can result in a power loss of anywhere between 50 to 80 percent. This is why you must ensure your panel is free from any shady spots; however, sometimes, it's not possible to keep it 100 percent shade-free.

Calculating the amount of solar energy theoretically available to you can help you figure out some cost estimates. There are also a few inefficiencies, such as shade, that you must consider to get a clearer view of your power production. As you estimate your costs, if things start becoming expensive, reevaluate by looking at your scope and developing a cost-effective solution. Aside from helping you estimate costs, these energy calculations can help you work out your solar panel array dimensions if you want to use one.

Step 3: Survey Your Site

A site survey helps you identify a suitable location to mount your solar panels. You want to get a spot that's shade-free for the best value and performance. Ask yourself: do you have somewhere in mind? Are there any objects nearby, such as trees or buildings that can shade your panel? Remember, this is a stand-alone system; if anything happens to or affects the solar panels, you will produce less energy than you need to run your house. Draw a rough sketch of your site to give you a clearer view of how things will look. Make sure to include the trees and buildings around you; even trees that are small right now might be something to worry about in a few years.

With solar thermal or hot water systems, shading doesn't cause as much power loss as with PV systems. If 10 percent of the panel is shaded, you lose the equivalent amount of power, 10 percent. However, with PV panels, even 5 percent shade can drop power production by over 80 percent. This drastic difference is caused by how the panels are constructed. A crystalline PV panel is made of individual solar cells that produce about 0.5V of potential energy. These cells are connected in series to increase their voltage output, so each panel contains more than one string of solar cells.

While connecting them in series increases their potential energy output, the panel is only as good as its weakest cell. This means if a cell produces a weak voltage, it compromises the whole system. This means if even one or two cells are covered by soft shade, they can reduce the output to something similar to what you would get on an overcast day. If they are covered by direct shade, this creates a bigger contrast, and the shaded cells short-circuit, causing the charge to flow in reverse.

The reversed cells absorb power disproportionately to what they produce. While they only produce 0.5V, they absorb 6 to 8V. This is what causes the drastic drop in power. If your panel contains a single string of cells, any short-circuits will affect the whole panel. If it has two strings, this means the output is halved. If you connect multiple solar panels in series, the effects of shading on one panel affects the output of the whole array. This reversal also causes heat production, which, if left unchecked, could cause it to burst into flames and get damaged.

If you are thinking of mounting your solar power system on a boat or RV, you need to find the right spot to mount the panels for them to receive optimal irradiance. Are you mounting them on the surface or using a structure to prop them up? Are they easy to get to clean and maintain? While it isn't a must for solar panels to be spotless, they need to be free of grime and dirt. These particles can accumulate over time, reducing the efficiency of your system.

Step 4: Select the Right Components and Work Out Full Costs

After a power and site analysis, you know how much power you need to generate and approximately how much it's going to cost you. The next step is thinking of the components you will use to build your system. These include solar panels, cabling, inverters, controllers, plugs, sockets, batteries, etc.

Step 5: Produce the Detailed Design

The design process can be complicated or simple based on the scope of the project. If you are merely installing a solar power system for lighting, for instance, you can complete the whole design pretty fast. If, instead, you are looking to install a solar electric system in your RV or boat, there's a lot more to consider, so the designing process will take longer. Whatever size your solar electric system is, whether you are planning to get an off-the-shelf solar kit or designing something from scratch, it is worth following this basic design process every time. It will ensure that you always get the best from your system.

Bringing Your Solar Power System to Life

After following all the steps, you have a viable design in hand. The next step is building a working model. The installation process will change according to your situation; for instance, putting a PV system on a home is different from installing one on an RV. However, despite these differences, the fundamental ideas and processes remain the same. Let's look at a few things you need to take care of before and during the installation process.

Permits and Planning Regulations

With respect to where you are in the world, there are different requirements and regulations for installing a solar energy system. While some countries have no regulation in place, some have stringent laws, and, in others, the law changes from state to state. Before you start putting together your solar system, you need to read up on local laws and regulations regarding solar power. You will also need two permits: an electrical and a building permit.

The permitting process requires that you collect specification sheets for all the products you want to use, document your design, and present all this information to the relevant building authorities. And although the actual permitting process varies from place to place, the information required is pretty consistent. Getting permits for both the electrical and mechanical elements of your solar power system is required and serves as a guarantee that the system you create will be safe for years to come.

You need to get the proper license and certifications before getting your permits or even thinking of installing a PV system. Even though you are not installing your off-grid system on a house, you still need to think about the mechanical and structural aspects of the solar power system. Before your permit can be issued, you have to prove that the solar array and the structure it's attached to is secure and can withstand the weight. Once all your permits and licenses are in place, you can get started.

PV Installation Safety

Installing a PV system can be a hazardous job. That's why you need to make sure you are wearing proper safety gear and following all safety protocols. Don't think that just because you are dealing with solar power, it doesn't pose the same electrical threat on-grid power poses! It does, so always keep that in mind. Additionally, you will probably be working on roofs and other areas with access to the elements; this makes things inherently more dangerous, so stay alert.

For many PV installations, the truly difficult part is installing the mechanical part of the PV system. Setting up the solar rack to hold the PV modules and evaluating how they will power everything can easily take up a huge chunk of the time you spend on this project. Most PV installations occur on rooftops. RV or boat rooftops are different from house rooftops, so you have to carefully consider the best way to attach the racking system to these roofs.

CHAPTER THREE

Electrical Terms and Tools

Since we are building an off-grid solar power system, it is battery-based, meaning it is stand-alone or independent of the grid. However, before we get started, having a good understanding of some fundamental electronic concepts will help you design and build the perfect PV system. This includes basic terminology and equations, as most of the terminology used is born from the electrical industry. Don't worry; I will try and keep the jargon to a minimum, so everything is easy to follow.

Here are a few electricity terms you should know:

Capacitor - an instrument that stores electrical charge, consisting of more than one conductor separated by an insulator. They are commonly used to filter out voltage spikes.

Charge controller - this is a device that determines how much energy should be transferred to the batteries for optimal performance and protects it from overcharging.

It is a crucial element since it determines the efficiency of the entire PV system and the batteries' operating lifespan.

Circuit - this is a loop of electrical flow, such as your lighting system or your air conditioning. For electricity to power a device or appliance, it has to flow in a completed circuit. A short circuit occurs when the flow of electricity is interrupted, like when a solar cell is covered by shade.

Circuit breaker - an instrument used to interrupt the flow of current in a circuit. To restore the current, the breaker must be reset after fixing whatever caused the overload or failure. Circuit breakers are utilized to protect circuits from overloads and short circuits.

Diode - this is a semiconducting device, such as a light-emitting diode that allows current to flow in one direction. For instance, diodes allow current to flow when the anode is positive in relation to the cathode.

Electric charge - this refers to the buildup of electric energy that occurs when electrons gather at either the positive or negative end of a cell. It is measured in coulombs and denoted as Q.

Electric current - this refers to the flow of electric charge from the positive end to the negative end and vice-versa. It's measured in amperes or amps (A), denoted as I.

Electrical energy - this represents the amount of work done by the current to flow through a circuit. It is measured in joules (J) and is denoted as E, even though 1 joule = 1 watt-second electrical energy is usually shown as watt-hours or kilowatt-hours.

Electric potential or voltage - this refers to the potential difference in electrical energy between two points, such as the positive and negative tips of a cell or battery. This difference is measured in volts, often denoted as V, and the greater the voltage, the higher the cell or battery's capacity.

Electrical power - this measures the rate of energy conversion. It defines work done by the current per unit time. The electrical power of a system is measured in watts (W), denoted as P. When buying appliances, you might see its power consumption denoted on the label. The higher the wattage, the more power/current the device consumes.

Fuse - this is another circuit interrupting device made of a strip of wire that melts if the current exceeds a certain amount. It basically creates a short circuit, and, to restore current, you have to replace the burnt fuse after correcting the problem.

Irradiance - this refers to the intensity of sunlight at a given moment. It is not to be confused with irradiation, which describes the quantity of solar energy generated over a particular duration, such as a few hours or a day.

Load - anything that consumes electrical energy such as appliances, lights, heaters, transformers, electric motors, etc.

Load center - this is where electrical loads get their power. Suppose you were getting power from a utility; in this case, the power would be sent to a single location, the main distribution panel (MDP), and then distributed throughout the building. In a photovoltaic system, the inverter provides the AC to the load center for distribution.

Resistance - this is the measure of opposition of flow current. A material such as gold, copper, or aluminum has very little resistance, and that makes them great conductors. However, materials such as rubber, wood, or plastic have very high resistance and restrict current flow. These materials make great insulators. Resistance is measured in ohms (Ω), denoted as R.

Resistor - a device made to resist current. It is made of a wire or carbon and controls the currents and voltages in the circuit, enabling the whole circuit to run smoothly. There are varying kinds of resistors, such as fixed and variable resistors.

Transistor - this is a device similar to a switch controlled by electrical signals. It can do two jobs: amplify and rectify. As an amplifier, it takes a tiny current at one end and produces a bigger current on the other end, the sort of thing you have in hearing aids or microphones. As a rectifier, it switches between low current and high current.

After going through these basic terms, it's important to understand how they relate to each other. Understanding current flow is crucial when measuring how much current will flow through your system. Voltage is a result of current and resistance.

I X R = V

This simple calculation is known as Ohm's law. It ignores the internal resistance and maximum current capacity of a power source such as a solar panel and focuses on the relationship between the voltage and current across and through the load. It comes in handy when dealing with resistors. If you only know two values of the equation, you can derive the missing value.

Voltage ÷ resistance = current

V ÷ R = I

Or

Voltage ÷ current = resistance

V ÷ I = R

Power is a product and time. For instance, a 5 V circuit with a 4-amp current produces 20 watts of power.

Volts x Current = Power

V x I = P

Alternatively, you can calculate power using current and resistance.

Current x resistance = Power

I2 x R = P

Similarly to voltage, you can derive a missing value if you know the other two values.

Direct Current and Alternating Current

There are two kinds of current that flow through a circuit: direct and alternating current. Direct current (DC) is a constant current that flows in one direction, moving from a high voltage point (positive) to a low voltage point (negative). PV modules produce DC current. When sunlight strikes the photovoltaic cells, the electrons flow from one direction through any load before heading back to the cells. It's also how electricity is stored in and produced from batteries. This makes it easy to charge batteries using PV modules because there is no inversion needed. The main disadvantage of DC electricity is it limits the distance the current can be transmitted before the current lost makes it inefficient. This means DC is great for short distances but transmitting it over long distances requires the use of large conductors.

Alternating current (AC) describes the flow of electric charge in the opposite direction. This direction reversal happens very rapidly, with current switching direction several times in a second. This helps it travel over long distances without losing a lot of current. This cycle of switching direction is referred to as frequency and is measured in Hertz (Hz). The faster the switching, the higher the frequency. Electricity on the grid is transmitted as AC, and most devices are calibrated to use AC. When designing your solar power system, you want to keep the current as low as possible. This way, the resistance doesn't increase, causing heat to build up, reducing the system's overall efficiency, and potentially putting your safety at risk. Resistance tends to build up over distance. So if you are transmitting current over a long distance, there's bound to be some heating and power loss.

Measuring Current

As you install your PV system, you will need to measure the DC output of an individual PV module or even an array to gauge its performance (its proper power output) or troubleshoot it if you suspect that it isn't working. You will also need to measure the AC output of the inverter for the same reasons. In either case, you will need an ammeter that can measure both DC and AC current. Another common reason to read the AC is to understand how much current an individual load is pulling. This is especially useful in battery-based systems like the one we are building. By knowing how much current each load needs, you can create a system large enough to accommodate your needs.

Before we look at ammeters, note that most inverters have a way to meter the AC output. These meters report on the system's power output, and although it is the same as metering current, it can be helpful. For instance, you can use this reported power value to calculate the value of the current.

Ammeter Types

There are two types of hand help ammeters: inline and clamp. Inline ammeters require current to flow through them to get a proper current reading. This means you have to connect the meter to the circuit to get a reading. Only use an inline meter to take current reading once you fully understand how the current is flowing through your system and how to disconnect and safely read the meter reading.

On the flip side, clamp ammeters have a jaw-like part that opens up, allowing you to place a part of the circuit in it to measure the current. This meter is a lot safer to use than the inline as no part of the circuit is exposed or connected to the meter. Clamp meters can also measure voltage and resistance, much like a digital multimeter, so investing in a good clamp meter is a great idea.

A lot of ammeters can handle measuring AC; however, they are limited when dealing with DC. Try and find a meter that can measure both AC and DC current and voltages. Also, make sure it can read DC levels high enough for the system you are building. For instance, get an ammeter that can read at least 100 amp DC (ADC); most are rated for about 10 ADC, which can make it difficult for you to measure the output of multiple arrays.

Taking a Current Reading

When taking a current reading, ensure that you are wearing protective gear, such as insulating gloves and safety glasses. Remember, a current is flowing, so there's a high chance that you might shock yourself, even though you are using a clamp meter. Next, verify that you can safely place the clamp around the conductor and avoid any live parts such as wire terminals, exposed conductors, fuse holders, etc. Some meters are auto-ranging, meaning they automatically set themselves to the proper range. However, if yours doesn't, set the dial to a value greater than the amount of current you expect to see. For most solar modules, this amount is between 10 ADC.

Before you start taking your reading, remember to always zero your meter (tare). This is because most meters measure a small amount of current even when not connected to anything like a circuit. By taring your meter, you are increasing its accuracy by giving it a baseline. Refer to the manufacturer's manual on how to zero out your meter. Once the meter is zeroed out, open the clamp and place it around a single conductor. If you place it around multiple conductors, it will read the sum of the current flowing through, which will not give you an accurate reading. Record the current value and remove the meter from the conductor.

Important tip: never connect an ammeter to two battery terminals. At best, you will ruin both the battery and the meter. That's because you will create a short circuit - furthermore, it is very dangerous.

Measuring Voltage

A voltage or electromotive force is the amount of push charged electrons have. Think of it as the pressure that encourages electrons to flow. In other words, voltage creates current. You will see this force often referred to as voltage potential because there needs to be a difference between the power source voltage and the load voltage for current to be created. For instance, for a PV array to charge a battery, it (the power source) needs to have more voltage than the battery (load). If the voltage is equal to or less than the battery, it cannot push the current into the battery meaning the battery won't get charged.

Photovoltaic systems contain both DC and AC voltages. While the principle concepts are the same, you need to ensure that you are using the correct voltage, and this will depend on which side of the PV system you are working on. These voltages are denoted as VDC for volts DC, and VSC for volts AC. This will help you distinguish the two when we are calculating voltages later on.

As we move on, you might come across the term nominal voltage. This refers to the baseline for measuring voltage. For a long time, most PV systems were available in one of two nominal voltages: 12V or 24V. This is because they were designed to charge batteries with nominal voltages of 6V and 12V. Another term you might come across is operating voltage. This is the voltage that pushes current into a load.

For a 12V nominal solar module, the operating voltage is somewhere between 17V and 18V. This means the cells in this particular module are wired to produce about 18V, which is enough to push current into a battery. So when you see me mention the voltage rating of a panel, I am referring to its nominal voltage. For grid-tie systems, nominal voltages have little influence on the system; however, they really come into play in stand-alone systems like ours. For your system to work, the PV array's nominal voltage must be high enough to charge the battery. The plainest way to ensure this happens is by having an array with the same nominal charge as the battery.

Taking a Voltage Reading

To take a voltage reading, you need a voltmeter or a digital multimeter. Getting a digital multimeter, such as a clamp meter, is more efficient and reduces the number of tools you'll need. When taking a voltage reading, there should be no load connected to the circuit. With no load, there's no current, and you can read the open-circuit voltage. Open circuit voltage is the voltage value of a circuit with no current flowing. This value allows you to verify the proper voltages in your system before switching the switches. Denoted as Voc, the value of this open-circuit voltage listed on a solar module is what is obtained in standard test conditions. When calculating how many modules to use with specific equipment, you need to use the Voc value to calculate the maximum circuit voltage.

The maximum circuit voltage or operating voltage, denoted as Vmp, is the highest voltage value the PV module or array can produce. Similar to the open-circuit voltage, the value of Vmp is affected by the temperature of the cells. Even though this value is used to indicate a PV module's operating voltage, the true operating voltage is lower because of the voltage loss that occurs as temperature increases. The Vmp value is linked to the current flowing between PV modules. When using Vmp, remember these two things: the voltage value drops as temperature increases, and PV modules need to always have a higher voltage to keep the current flowing.

When taking a voltage reading: start by wearing your protective gear and ensure no current is flowing. Always keep in mind that PV modules are considered live whenever they are exposed to the sun. So, just because the current isn't flowing, it doesn't mean you can't get shocked; you might complete the circuit and cause current to flow through you. Next, make the position where you want to take your reading accessible, then place the black meter lead on the connection point labeled common, and the red meter lead in the point labeled V. It can also be labeled Ω, meaning it can also measure resistance. Set the dial to the appropriate DC voltage range, then place the black lead on the PV module's negative terminal and the red one on the positive terminal and read your voltage reading.

Important tip: after taking your voltage reading, switch the leads and note the presence of the negative symbol. This indicates reverse polarity, which means the voltage from the source is connected backwards to the meter. This short test can help you when troubleshooting your system.

Measuring Resistance

In an electrical circuit, resistance affects the flow of current. If a material has a high resistance, little or no current can flow through it. These materials are referred to as insulators. Conductors are the opposite: they have low resistance and allow current to flow freely. In a PV system, you want as little resistance as possible, and the conductor used in your system has the biggest influence on this. The bigger the conductor, the more the room electrons have to move around, which results in less resistance. Think of the conductor as a highway and the electrons as cars. The more lanes the highway has, the more cars that can travel and vice-versa.

Taking a Resistance Reading

When installing your PV system, you need to check the resistance in the circuits. This means determining the resistance in the wires you will run from the solar array to the inverter or battery bank. Taking a resistance reading will help you verify if the wires you are using will allow current to flow and make sure they are properly connected to the electrical equipment. The simplest way to determine the circuit's resistance is to calculate the total voltage drop across the circuit using Ohm's Law. When there's resistance, the voltage at the source will be higher than the voltage at the load.

As with all other tests, start by putting on your protective gear and switch on the AC and DC disconnects, stopping any current flow. Make the area where you are going to take your resistance reading accessible. This means opening the covers to the disconnects and inverters. Next, place the black meter lead on the connection labeled common, and the red lead on the connection labeled Ω. Now set your digital multimeter to read the resistance of the circuit. Always start with the highest resistance values on your meter. If you need more exact readings, you can set the dial to smaller numbers. Alternatively, you can use an auto-ranging meter that will set itself automatically.

Now place the black lead on the first connection point typically found inside a disconnect and the red lead on the other end of the conductor. Read the meter reading or listen for the alarm, which indicates a low-resistance connection. If the alarm doesn't ring as you expect it to, you may have made the wrong connection or placed the lead in the wrong spot. Once you are done taking your resistance reading, remove the leads from the duel and pull them from the meter.

Ohm's Law: Connecting Current, Voltage, and Resistance

After going through these basic terms, it's important to understand how they relate to each other. As we proceed with this project, you will use all three components in your calculations. Understanding how they relate to each other is crucial to coming up with a successful design. Understanding current flow is vital when measuring how much current will flow through your system. Voltage is a result of current and resistance.

$$I \times R = V$$

This simple calculation is known as Ohm's Law. It ignores the internal resistance and maximum current capacity of a power source such as a solar panel and focuses on the relationship between the voltage and current across and through the load. It comes in handy when gauging conductor sizes, calculating power, and figuring out the voltage drop. If you know two values of the equation, you can derive the missing value.

Voltage ÷ resistance = current

V ÷ R = I

Or

Voltage ÷ current = resistance

V ÷ I = R

Power vs. Energy

In a PV system, all anyone is ever interested in is how much power can the system produce? However, most people don't realize what this means and how closely related energy and power are, often misusing the two terms. To achieve a successful install, you need to properly grasp the difference between power and energy. Power is a rate; it's a product of voltage and current measured in watts.

Volts x Current = Power

V x I = P

For instance, a 5 V circuit with a 4-amp current produces 20 watts of power. Unlike regular rates, power doesn't have a typical time value tied to it, as you would normally see on other rates. But it does; 1 watt = 1 joule of energy per second (that's the time value). Energy, however, is a quantity, a measurement of power multiplied by time. It's measured in kilowatt-hours, and this is the value your utility company charges you for. Simply put, it's the quantity of energy a load consumes in a given time. When it comes to PV systems, people tend to focus on the power value rather than the energy value, which is what actually makes the difference.

You want to keep your eye on the energy value because it can help you determine how much everything will cost. For example, suppose you install your system in a place that doesn't produce enough energy consistently. In that case, you will have to supplement this by buying energy from a utility company. The power equation can help you determine your array's power output or even calculate the amount of current your inverter will produce if you know the operating voltage and power values. Here's a simple graphic showing both Ohm's Law and the power equation. It will come in handy when making our calculations later on.

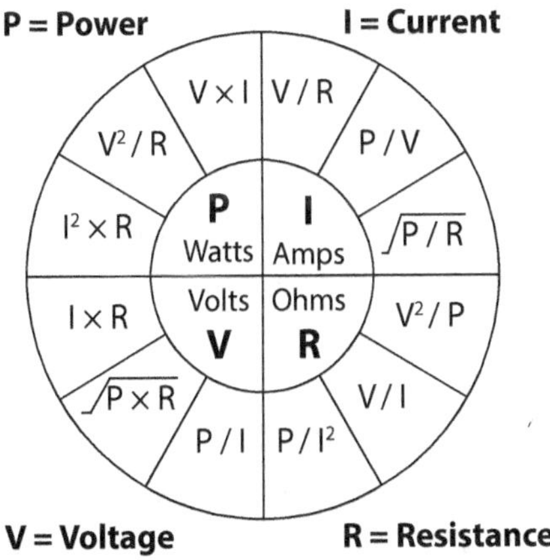

If you know the amount of power an array will produce, you can calculate this energy production. Find out how many hours the PV will be operating, then multiply this value by the power. That is:

Power(in watt/kilowatt) x number of sun hours = Energy (in watt-hours or kilowatt-hours).

Remember, there's a big difference between watts and kilowatts, so keep your units straight.

When using batteries, their energy output is rated in amp-hours because it's focused on the current flow, not the power flow. Amp-hours describe the quantity of electrons that flow in a given time. To convert watt-hours to amp-hours and vice-versa, simply divide the watt-hours value by the voltage.

Watt-hours (Wh) ÷ Voltage (V) = Amp-hours (Ah)

Circuit Configurations

When wiring your PV system, you will configure it in a way that delivers the desired voltage and current reading. You can configure a circuit in two ways: series and parallel. Each configuration affects both current and voltage differently.

- **Series configuration** - here, connections are made by connecting the positive end to the negative end and so on, but the number of modules that can be connected this way is limited. Connecting a group of modules in series creates a series string of modules. Think of it as a daisy chain. In a series connection, the voltages are additive while the current value remains the same. For instance, if you had five modules, each rated 12V and 4A, connected in series, the voltage reading would be 60V (5 x 12V), but the current reading would still remain 4A. To calculate the power output of such an array, simply multiply the voltage and current values.

60V x 4A = 240W

- **Parallel configuration** - here, the connections are complementary to series connections. Instead of connecting the positive end of one module to the negative end of the other, you connect it to the positive end of the next module. Likewise, negative ends are connected to negative ends. This type of connection maintains a constant voltage value, but the current values are additive. Using the same example as above, the array's voltage reading will be 12V, but the current value would be 20A (4A x 5). The power output, however, is unchanged:

12V x 20A = 240W

If the power outputs of both connections are the same, then which connection type is better? The answer depends on the current and voltage rating of the components you use.

- Series-parallel configuration - most PV systems use a combination of both series and parallel connections. If you have two strings of five modules, they are connected in series to increase the voltage; and wired in parallel to increase their current output. The resulting array has the following ratings.

5 x 12V = 60V

2 strings in parallel x 4A = 8A

60V x 8A = 480W

CHAPTER FOUR

Solar System Components

With this basic understanding of a few electrical terms, let's take a look at the components of the photovoltaic system we are building. While each system is unique, all of them contain several common components. These components differ based on your needs and the local regulations. Let's dive in.

Pv Modules

Before you go installing a solar panel, it pays to know how it works. Once you understand the science behind it, you can easily get it to do what you need and sort out any issues that come along. A photovoltaic module - which is also called a solar panel - is an assembly of solar or PV cells. This device traps the sun's energy and converts it into electricity. Thi electricity is produced when photons from the sun excite the electrons in the PV cell. On its own, a solar cell doesn't produce much electricity; however, when bundled together, these modules form larger electrical units that produce a lot more electricity.

Solar cells are made from silicon; however, pure silicon is more of an insulator rather than a conductor. For it to produce electricity, it has to allow the flow of electrons; that's why it is doped during the manufacturing process with boron and phosphorus. In the production of semiconductors, doping is the deliberate induction of impurities into an intrinsic semiconductor to change its electrical, optical, or structural properties. The doped element referred to as an external semiconductor acts more like a conductor than a semiconductor.

The introduction of dopants supplements electrons and electron holes to the silicone molecule. The phosphorus atoms have more electrons, while the boron has more electron holes waiting to be filled with electrons. The phosphorus-doped side of the cell becomes known as the n-type (the side facing the sun), while the boron-doped side is the p-type (the side facing away from the sun). When the sunlight hits the n-types side, the extra electrons from the phosphorus become excited and are more than willing to flow to the electron holes in the boron-doped side given a proper path.

This path, also referred to as the p-n junction, acts as a diode allowing the electrons to move from the positive side to the negative side. This means for electrons to flow from the n-type side to the p-type side, they must go through a circuit. As more electrons flow through the circuit to the positive side, more electrons from the boron-doped side are pushed through the p-n junction to the negative side. This process continues indefinitely as long as there's sunlight.

Solar Panel Types

The solar power market has grown rapidly, and manufacturers are producing new technologies to make harvesting energy from the sun a lot easier. While the end product is still the same, these different technologies have their pros and cons. Let's take a look at each one.

Crystalline Solar Cells

These are the oldest types of solar cells. The main reason they are used so often is because they have a high-efficiency rating. There are two kinds of crystalline solar cells; monocrystalline and poly or multi-crystalline. Monocrystalline PV cells begin as a molten vat of boron-doped silicon. A starter seed, a crystal measuring 4 inches by 2 inches, is introduced to the doped silicon and becomes the base structure of the cells. During the production process, the silicon aligns itself with the starter seed taking its exact shape and structure. The seed is then removed from the mixture, and a crystal grows around it, forming an ingot measuring 6 to 8 inches. The ingot is pulled from the molten vat until it reaches the desired height, about 6 feet.

The cylindrical ingot is then sliced into very thin wafers that are exposed to phosphorous vapors in the diffuser for the second step of the doping process. At this point, the photovoltaic cells are complete, and an electrical grip can be placed on top to allow electrons to flow. Monocrystalline PV cells are more efficient than polycrystalline cells because their molecular structure is uniform from top to bottom. This allows the sun's photons to move the greatest number of electrons because the cells are aligned and facing the same direction. Monocrystalline PV cells start out as circular wafers; however, since PV modules are rectangular, the cells are squared off to fit the module. They are cut into octagons which allows them to be densely packed in a module frame reducing the amount of dead space. This octagonal shape allows the cells to be densely packed but isn't putting the cells right next to each other.

Polycrystalline cells are manufactured differently from monocrystalline ones. With monocrystalline cells, the ingots are circular. Here, however, they are brick-shaped or cubed. The manufacturing process begins at the molten boron-silicon vat, but instead of pulling a crystal, the silicon mixture is formed in a cubic crucible which causes the silicone mixture to cool, forming multiple crystals. After the ingot has cooled, it's sliced into thin wafers and doped with phosphorus vapors. Once the cells are formed, an electrical grid is added, and the modules are ready.

Due to the multiple crystalline structures in these cells, the photons have a harder time releasing the electrons. This results in a reduction in their efficiency. On the flip side, these cells are packed right next to one another, reducing the amount of dead space even further.

This gives them a power rating per unit area similar to monocrystalline modules even though their efficiency per cell is reduced.

Thin-film Cells

Aside from crystalline PV tech, there are other PV technologies in use. The term thin-film is a general term for several different technologies that use thin films of material to create solar panels. Even though different materials are used, at the base level all thin-film technologies deposit a material that can produce a photovoltaic effect onto a backing material referred to as a substrate. The name thin-film comes from the fact that the PV material deposited on the substrate is very thin, ranging from nanometers to a few micrometers thick. A human hair is about 100 micrometers thick, while these thin-films are 250 micrometers thick. This means they are about as thick as the size of 2 ½ human hairs.

Amorphous silicon - Denoted as aSI, this is a pretty common type of PV thin-film module. It is based on technology that deposits silane gas on a substrate. One of the many advantages of aSI is its ability to be added on nonrigid substrates such as vinyl or PVC roofing material. These aSI PV modules have become very popular for use on large commercial flat roofs despite having less power per unit area when compared to crystalline modules (about 50 to 60 percent). Its ability to be incorporated into roofing material makes it a very attractive option in terms of aesthetics and overall cost.

These aSI modules can be manufactured in different shapes, helping them accommodate any application. For instance, they can be made to stick on a metal roof or become part of the roofing material. Even though these modules are not as power dense as the crystalline kind, they can use sunlight even at low light levels, such as early in the morning or late in the evening. This gives them an increased energy output as compared to crystalline modules.

Cadmium telluride - Another popular thin-film material is cadmium telluride (CdTe). To construct a cadmium telluride PV module, a thin layer of CdTe is deposited on a substrate. A common substrate used is glass, and the CdTe later is placed between two glass sheets to protect the cells. This glass-on-glass process means that CdTe modules can be used in place of regular glass windows allowing light to enter while generating electricity. A big advantage of CdTe modules is the relatively low cost of the raw materials; this has made the price of the technology relatively low and competitive. That said, one of the raw materials used, tellurium, is a rare element meaning large-scale production might be problematic.

Copper indium gallium diselenide (CIGS) - This material used four different raw materials to create a substance that can be deposited on both rigid and nonrigid substrates. Even though this technology has existed for a long time, it has only recently gained traction because it can make PV films nanometers thick while other materials require about a micrometer of material to work with. This means CIGS modules use less raw material, which reduces manufacturing costs. This technology has been incorporated into emerging roofing installations, with the cells being made into cylinders rather than traditional rectangular modules. This tubular format allows the cells to be perpendicular to the sun for more hours in a day, thus increasing energy production.

Now that you understand the different PV technologies available, how do you choose the best? For most applications, crystalline panels work best, giving you reasonable value for money. Thin-film panels can be a great choice for smaller installations where space isn't an issue, but they are not practical for generating more than a couple of hundred watts of power because of their overall size. You would need to cover a large area with thin-film for it to produce enough power.

When looking for a solar panel, the first thing you have to ask yourself is how long you want to use this panel? For instance, if you want something that lasts ten to twenty years, it's best to go with quality branded products over unbranded ones. This is because a cheaper one might not live up to your expectations. Understand that not all solar panels are created equal, so if you are looking for something to power your RV, boat, or caravan, your requirements are modest, meaning even a cheap solar panel can work out.

Most people associate cheap solar panels with poor quality products because, in the past, they were poorly assembled and were a recipe for disaster. But thanks to advancements in technology and better manufacturing processes, you can get a cheap solar panel online that is reliable enough to last anywhere between five to ten years. When purchasing a solar panel from an unknown manufacturer, follow these tips:

- Get a panel bigger than what you think you'll need - if you are buying a cheap PV panel, you are most likely saving about 50 percent off on the price. Despite this save, expect it to degrade more quickly than a branded panel would. Also, it might not be as productive as a quality panel. To counter this loss of efficiency, you can purchase a panel that has a higher watt rating than what you actually need. Aim for about 15 to 20 percent more power output. This way, you are assured it will produce enough power.
- Warranty - where branded panels have a warranty of about ten to twenty years, most cheap panels have a warranty of about one or two years. When purchasing the panel, take time to go over the warranty agreement and understand what it offers. Look for a warranty that assures a minimum output under controlled conditions, about 80 percent of the quoted amount under controlled conditions.
- Glass - a major issue with most cheap panels is leakage. Go for panels made from tempered or toughened glass because it's eight times stronger than regular glass. If the glass covering the panel is chipped, it can cause a significant drop in power output as well as allow water to get into the panel, causing a short circuit.

Battery Packs

PV panels rarely power loads directly because the power collected by the module varies depending on the strength of the sun. The varying power source can be too much for most electrical equipment to deal with. For stand-alone systems, you need to store the power produced by the PV array in batteries which allows for a steady power source and increases the flexibility of your energy use. There are several battery types that can be used to store solar energy. Traditionally, deep-cycle lead-acid batteries were used. They are similar to regular car batteries but have a different internal design that allows them to be massively discharged and recharged numerous times over.

Many lead-acid batteries are either 6V or 12V, similar to most PV panels, but they can be connected together to create a battery bank, which creates a bigger energy store. When connected in series, these batteries increase their overall voltage output keeping the current fixed, but when connected in parallel, the current increases while the voltage remains constant. More recently, thanks to advancements in technology, lithium-based batteries have become available for use with solar systems. Let's take a deeper look at both technologies.

Lead-acid Batteries

These batteries are popular with solar systems because of their relatively low cost, strong design, and capacity to reach a high depth of discharge. The batteries are available as flooded and valve-regulated versions. Flooded lead-acid batteries have a liquid electrolyte inside that floods the cells. They have removable caps on each cell that allow you to check the liquid level, adding distilled water when levels start falling. Flooded lead-acid batteries work very well in stand-alone systems where batteries are cycled regularly. They are able to hold up better than their sealed counterparts.

Flooded batteries are more cost-effective for stand-alone systems, and the additional maintenance is offset by the lengthened battery life. They require a high client interaction and maintenance level if you want them to last as long and perform well. This is because hydrogen gas is produced during the charge and discharge process, reducing the amount of water in the battery. Since these batteries need to remain immersed in a liquid to perform optimally, you need to periodically add water to replace the lost liquid. When properly maintained, a flood lead-acid battery can last for well over ten years.

You also need to periodically intentionally overcharge it. This process involves increasing the charging voltage to stir up the electrolyte solution and scrub the sulfation (corrosion) that accumulates on the plates. This process generates a lot of hydrogen gas so you might smell rotten eggs. Every battery manufacturer has their own recommendations for when you should perform this overcharge or equalization charge. An equalization charge must be performed in a controlled manner. Unless you are qualified, you should let a professional handle it. Hydrogen is a highly flammable gas and could ignite if care is not taken.

Valve Regulated Lead-acid Batteries (VRLA)

The other kind of lead-acid batteries are valve-regulated batteries, also known as sealed lead-acid batteries. They are closed off from their environment and have no internal components for you to maintain. Even though the battery is sealed off, the valves allow it to release hydrogen gas when necessary. As the battery charges, the chemical process causes the release of hydrogen, which increases the battery's internal pressure. When the gas pressure gets to a specific level, the valve opens, and the gas is released.

VRLAs are quite popular in both grid-tie and battery-based PV systems. They are generally not cycled regularly since, in most locations, the grid is stable, and there are few power outages. This means the battery stays fully charged. While this might not hurt the battery, it needs to be cycled every three to six months to help increase its lifespan. VRLAs don't need as much maintenance as flooded lead-acid batteries because they don't require you to top up the liquid. This has led to the nickname maintenance-free batteries, but this isn't entirely true. You still need to monitor and evaluate its performance regularly. They also produce less hydrogen, which makes placing them easier because the venting requirements are less restrictive. This means you can easily stack VRLAs together, whereas flooded lead-acid batteries would require a lot of floor space.

While VRLAs are great, they do have some downsides. First, they cannot accept excessive charge like flooded lead-acid batteries. That's because the battery might produce more hydrogen when exposed to higher voltages which it might not be able to release to maintain its safety levels. VRLAs require proper charging as per the manufacturer's instructions and proper monitoring to ensure proper voltage levels are maintained. Secondly, these battery types also have a very short lifespan even when properly maintained. A typical lifespan for VRLAs is about seven years, but improper use and a lack of maintenance can make one go bad in less than a year. Basically, flooded lead-acid batteries are hardier than VRLAs. Lastly, they are more expensive than their counterparts.

Lead-calcium Batteries

These batteries have calcium added to the active material instead of antimony. The addition of calcium reduces the water consumption making the plates more resistant to corrosion and decreases the battery's self-discharge rate. Despite all these advantages, these batteries are way pricier than regular lead-acid batteries, and very few deep cycle batteries are made, making them less popular than normal batteries. Just like lead-acid batteries, though, they come in both flooded and valve-regulated options. Their battery capacity ranges from 6V to 12V, but this will depend on the manufacturer and the battery size.

Nickel-cadmium Batteries

Instead of lead, nickel oxide hydroxide and cadmium are used as base materials for the negative and positive plates.

Often called NiCd batteries, they provide less voltage per cell, meaning you would have to connect more cells in series to achieve this voltage. For instance, a 12V NiCd battery has about ten cells. Even though they are not typically used in photovoltaic systems, they can be excessively discharged with no adverse effects on the battery. This gives the battery more cycles in its lifespan. However, despite this obvious advantage, these batteries are very expensive and don't react well to cold temperatures, meaning they need to be stored in a temperature-controlled environment to perform properly. Additionally, you also have to adjust the charge set-points for the chargers because of the voltage differences linked to NiCd batteries.

AGM Deep Cycle Batteries

Absorbed glass mat (AGM) batteries are a kind of lead-acid battery traditionally used in cars. Initially developed for military use, the deep cycle batteries were favored for their durability in extreme conditions and high performance. Over the years, their use has extended to cars, RVs, boats, and solar power storage. Unlike regular lead-acid batteries, the absorbed glass mat allows for more power to be packed into the lead-acid battery housing. These batteries are vibration resistant making them great for use on boats; they are a lot more resilient to cycling than flooded batteries. Since they are not flooded, they cannot leak in case of damage, so you can mount them in any orientation without worrying about leakage. The biggest difference between AGMs and other lead-acid batteries is the level of maintenance needed. These batteries are sealed, meaning you never have to check on the water levels, so you install them and never check on them until your scheduled maintenance check date.

Thanks to advancements in technology, AGMs have become quite popular in the solar power storage market. These deep cycle AGM batteries, such as the Tesla Powerwall or the LG Chem RESU, are designed to keep up with the high energy demands and outputs of the solar panels. They are handy for small off-grid PV systems such as powering your RV, camper, or boat. Their low maintenance, high durability, and relatively low upfront costs make them a great choice for your PV system. If you are thinking about which battery type to pick, I would recommend going for AGM batteries because they offer the best energy storage and they're low maintenance.

Lithium-ion Batteries

Lithium-ion batteries are a lot smaller in size than typical lead-acid batteries. Despite being smaller, they have superior energy density giving them more charge capacity, which has made them quite popular. Lithium-ion batteries are considered the most cost-effective and reliable battery types you can use in a PV system. These batteries have several advantages over typical lead-acid batteries. As I mentioned before, they are smaller and lighter than lead-acid batteries of the same capacity. This size reduction is due to its superior energy density and increased capacity. They can also be deeply discharged to about 80 or 90 percent of their total capacity without damaging the battery itself. Lead-acid batteries are not as tolerant of this type of roughhousing and can easily get damaged or discharged below their state of charge, or discharged faster than their discharge rate. This causes the batteries to lose potential cycles. If you are seeking an easy to maintain, cost-effective battery option, then lithium-ion is the way to go.

Charge Controller

If you are using batteries, you will need a charge controller to manage electricity flow in and out of the battery. The charge controller takes DC power produced by the PV panel and directs it to the batteries. Its main function is controlling the power that goes into the batteries; this way, they won't overcharge or get damaged. This regulation function has led some people to refer to them as regulators. Charge controllers regulate voltage and current according to charge set points. Each manufacturer publishes its own charge set-points so you can optimally charge your battery to maximize its life span.

Here's a breakdown of how the controller works during the charging process.

- Bulk charging - this is the first stage of the charging process, and it happens first thing in the morning after the batteries have been drained the previous night. Bulk charging pushes as many amps into the battery and raises the voltage in the process. Think of it this way: bulk charging is like trying to fill a large glass from a tap. The battery's voltage is the water level in the glass; if it gets too low, you need to allow as much current as you can into the battery to push it back up. That is, open the tap all the way. In this example, the charge controller is the tap.

The PV array and tap are limited in the flow they can provide; however, as long as the energy levels are low the glass, or battery will accept all the current it can get. As more current flows in, the voltage level rises and will continue to do so until it reaches a predetermined level referred to as the bulk voltage set point. After that, the flow will slow down because it can't accept any more charge. If the flow isn't regulated, the current generates heat which can damage the battery.

The exact bulk voltage set point is determined by the manufacturer. Some batteries, such as lithium-ion, have higher charge set points than others, so you have to ensure your charge controller is set to the right voltage. If a battery is consistently charged over its bulk charge point, its life span is significantly reduced.

- Absorption charging - the second stage of the charging process is absorption charging. After bringing the battery up the bulk voltage set point, it cannot take any more charge. Forcing it to will cause the release of more hydrogen gas than can release safely, which is dangerous. However, the battery is only about 80 percent full at this point, and the absorption charge will top it off. Remember our metaphor of the glass; the tap was fully open; the glass didn't get full because the force of the water pushed some of the water over the top. This means that the glass isn't 100 percent full. During the absorption charge stage, the charge controller steadies the voltage and reduces the current sent into the battery. This allows the battery to charge to 100 percent.

Normally charging a battery to its full capacity takes hours, with the exact amount of time depending on the battery's capacity and the array. Throughout the day, the charge controller automatically starts and stops the charging stages.

- Floating charge - this is the final stage of charging, and it's meant to keep the battery at full capacity after the absorption stage. Since the PV array has a limited amount of time to charge the battery, the controller only enters the floating charge stage after the other two stages are complete, and there's enough charge left to send a float charge to the battery. With a limited number of peak sun hours, such as during winter, the controller might have a hard time getting the battery fully charged. This means the battery might be drained very low due to its increased use.

While most small-scale charge controllers are only charge regulators, others have additional features that help them work with larger systems. These features include:

Load control - for systems that support DC loads, such as stand-alone or battery-based systems such as ours, the charge controller uses the load control feature to ensure the batteries are not excessively discharged. This feature pulls electricity directly from the battery to the lead through the controller, and, as the load runs, the reducing battery capacity is monitored by the controller. If the load runs too long and the controller detects that the battery charge levels have dropped, it cuts off electricity flow to the load. This ensures the load doesn't drain the battery too much - if it did drain too much, it could be damaged. This feature also keeps the load cut off until power levels are back to a particular level, protecting the battery from damage.

Auxiliary load control - in instances where you need loads to run or when there's excess charge or the battery needs attention, the auxiliary load control can come in handy. Auxiliary loads enhance safety or performance. For instance, fans connected to flooded battery banks. When charged to a particular point, the batteries release hydrogen gas, which is flammable. When this feature is activated, power is sent to a fan that fans the hydrogen out of the room. Another example is the warning lights or alarms that come on when your battery's excessively drained.

Status meters - these allow you to monitor your system by displaying various parameters such as battery capacity, voltage levels, current levels, etc. Other more sophisticated meters monitor energy values in and out of the battery. Knowing how many amp-hours you have can be very useful in a battery-based system.

Inverter

If the solar modules are the heart of the system in a PV system, then the inverter is the brains. An inverter takes the DC produced by the modules and converts it into AC to be used around the home. Not only that, but these devices can also detect when a utility is gone and when batteries need attention. That's pretty impressive. The inverter has the following tasks converting DC to AC; ensuring the cycle of AC is 60 cycles, reducing voltage variations, and ensuring the AC waveform created is suitable for the intended use.

There are two kinds of inverters: utility-interactive inverters and stand-alone inverters. Utility-interactive inverters are divided into two groups, namely, grid direct and battery-based, while stand-alone inverters are battery-based. Normally, in a stand-alone system, the inverter takes power from the battery bank and converts it into AC power. It then delivers it to the load connected to the main distribution panel. As long as the capacity of the battery remains high enough, the inverter will continue powering the loads. Once the battery discharges to the level you set it to, the inverter alerts you to start a generator, or it can automatically start one to prevent the batteries from excessively discharging and getting damaged.

When the generator connects to the inverter, the latter stops drawing DC power from the battery to make AC and starts distributing the generator's power through to the load, also charging the batteries with the remaining available power. The built-in charger performs a multistage charging cycle similar to a charge controller. Most systems are set up to allow the batteries to deep discharge before getting assistance from the generator, so the cycle takes several hours to charge the battery bank fully. When the batteries are full again, you can turn the generator off, enabling the inverter to go back to its regular job of powering loads through the battery bank.

Inverters in a battery-based system are the workhorses of the system. They are made to work in different environments and deliver high-quality power. Most act as inverters and chargers. The safety features built into them keep the battery from deeply discharging by alerting you to a low battery situation and then proceeding to start a generator or shut down. As a charger, it ensures the battery goes through the multistage charging process.

Unlike grid-direct inverters, they don't have ground fault protection, but they can be added to the system. They also have disconnects and overcurrent protection, and an interface that allows you to program the system. Inverters come in various sizes, with most starting from 1 kW of AC output to about 6 kW. For systems that need more power than one inverter can provide, they are often stacked together or connected in a configuration that provides more AC output. For instance, you can stack individual inverters to provide up to 36 kW.

CHAPTER FIVE

Putting it All Together

Having taken a look at the basic components of a photovoltaic system, let's put them all together. We are putting together an off-grid PV system, and unlike a grid-tie system, there's no backup electricity from the grid to help you out in case the system malfunctions. This means you have to be more vigilant as you set up your system.

Step 1: Calculate how Much Power you will Need

You wouldn't plan a road trip without knowing how far you are going to travel, right? This way, you can calculate how much gas you need. The same applies to your PV system. You can't go off and buy five solar panels and a battery pack and hope that's all you will need. That's foolhardy; after all, that system is providing all the power to your RV or camper, and you can't be sure it's enough to power everything you need. To determine how much power you need, you have to factor in all the power and energy consumption of the loads you intend to use.

Start by identifying all the components you will need to power and the total Watts-hours needed. You will make a similar table to the one in Chapter Two when we looked at how to calculate the amount of energy you will need.

Here's an example:

Device	Wattage	Voltage	Hours used daily	Watt-hours
Lighting	11W	12V	4	44Wh
Small fridge	12W	12V	24	288Wh
TV	40W	12V	3	120Wh
Laptop	40W	12V	6	240Wh
Phone charging	5W	12V	4	20Wh
Other loads	2W	12V	24	48Wh
Total energy consumption				760Wh

When figuring out what loads your system will need to power, here are a few pointers to keep in mind for systems powered entirely by battery banks.

- In many situations, the water pump is the main water source in your home, RV, boat, or camper. These pumps, though, are large electrical loads that can quickly drain your battery and cause problems for the inverter.
- When sizing your system, ensure you incorporate every electrical load you can imagine.
- Never forget to factor in phantom loads. These small loads are often on 24/7 and can even draw power when they are off. If left unchecked, they

can quickly drain your battery pack and cause major problems. For instance, if these loads are always present, you can't turn off your inverter, meaning the inverter is always going to have to supply them with power. This means that the inverter has to consume some power to provide the power needed. Therefore, it operates at its worst efficiency level, and that can be dangerous, especially when dealing with larger loads. The solution to this is turning off phantom loads and allowing the inverter to rest so it can operate optimally.

- That said, never place anything that uses electricity to generate heat on a battery-powered system. These loads, also referred to as resistive loads, can quickly drain your battery, so this rules out using things such as water heaters, electric stoves, etc.

After getting the total watt-hours from the appliances, calculate the watt-hours needed per day from the PV modules. Multiply the entire energy consumption per day by 1.3 to account for the energy loss in the system. As per our example

760 x 1.3 = 988

You will need your PV modules to produce about 988 Wh to sufficiently power the system.

Step 2: Calculating Your Battery Needs

After calculating how much power you need, you should figure out how much battery capacity you need to store this energy. The batteries used in PV systems are deep-cycle batteries specially designed to discharge to low power levels and rapidly recharge every day for years. The battery bank you create should be large enough to operate all your appliances at night and on cloudy days. To calculate the total ampere hours you need to:

- Start by calculating your total energy consumption in watt-hours per day.
- Then divide this figure by 0.85 to accommodate for energy loss in the battery.
- Then divide the result by 0.6 for the depth of discharge.
- Divide the answer you get by the nominal voltage of the battery
- Then multiply the answer with days you need the system to operate when the PV system produces no power (days of autonomy) to get the required Ah of the battery.

Here's the formula:

Battery Capacity (Ah) = {Total Watt-hours used daily / (0.85 x 0.6 x the battery's nominal voltage)} x Days of autonomy.

If we have a 12V battery that's meant to run for about two days of autonomy then as per the example:

Our total watt-hours per day = 760Wh

(760/ (0.85 x 0.6 x 12)) x 2

760/0.85 = 894. 11

894.11/ 0.6 = 1490.20

1490.20 / 12 = 124.18

124.18 x 2 = 248.37

You will need to get a battery bank with a capacity of 248.37 Ah.

If you are using any DC appliances, you also have to include them in your energy calculations. You will make the same calculations as you did with the AC devices, but keep the numbers separate because, for AC loads, you have to account for the efficiency losses linked to the conversion of DC to AC. After taking those losses into account, you can add the totals together to get your final energy consumption value. The inverter is also a load, and, while it's not a large load, it can still significantly throw your system sizing math off if you don't account for it. You can find out how much energy the inverter draws from the manufacturer's specification sheet, then add this to your total.

As you calculate your battery bank size, remember this is a stand-alone system, so no other source of power exists. This bank is the primary source of energy, so as you size the system, here are a few things that dictate the battery's capacity:

The Efficiency of the Inverter

When converting DC to AC, there is always some energy loss expected, which is why no inverter can deliver 100 percent of the power from the battery bank to the loads.

That said, if the inverter is efficient, you won't need a battery bank with a large capacity as more energy will be converted. When picking an inverter, consider the loads and its size so as to maximize its efficiency. What this means is - don't use a 4kW inverter when you only draw about 1kW.

Inverter efficiencies are listed on the specifications sheets; however, the value denoted here shows the inverter's peak efficiency, so it will be an impressive value, something close to 95 percent. In reality, however, achieving 95 percent efficiency daily is hard, so most inverters actually have an efficiency of about 90 percent.

How Many Days You Should Expect the Battery Bank to Last Without Recharging

Also referred to as days of autonomy, these are the days you want the battery bank to sustain the electrical needs. That is the number of days you expect the battery bank to provide power without recharging. This number will depend on your needs and the climate of the surrounding area. But typically, the more autonomy days you want, the more batteries you will need and the higher the cost of the system will be. Most stand-alone systems can go for about two to three days.

Its Operating Temperature and Voltage

The battery's temperature affects its capacity; the colder the battery gets, the less power it can provide. This is because the cold temperatures affect the chemical reactions going on in the battery. The colder the storage room, the more batteries you will need. For instance, if temperatures dip below freezing point, you will need three batteries for every two that you would use in a warmer place. You might think that hot temperatures won't affect the battery, but they do. Hot temperatures can cause the internal pressure of the battery to increase, which can be incredibly dangerous.

The amount of energy drawn from a battery is referred to as depth of discharge (DOD). Often denoted as a percentage, the higher the DOD, the more energy drawn from the bank. As with days of autonomy, the DOD of the system should be dictated in your system design because it affects the battery bank's overall size. Most battery specification sheets show the number of cycles vs. DOD in a chart. You can utilize this data to estimate the amount of power a battery bank can deliver.

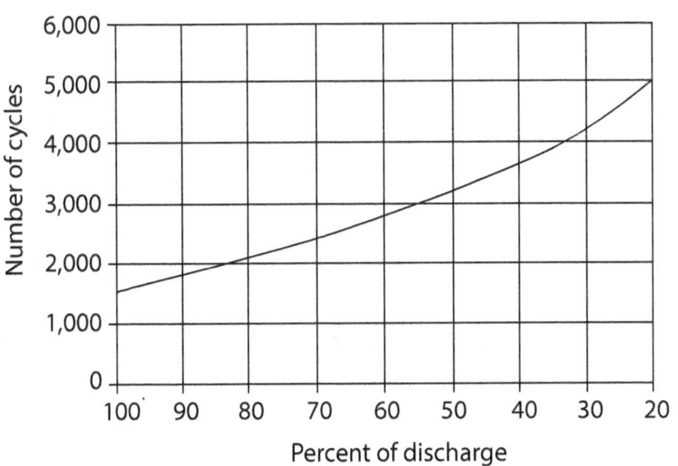

The above graph shows a battery's cycles vs. it's DOD.

The smaller the DOD, the higher the number of cycles. This doesn't mean that a lower DOD delivers more power. Let's say you have a battery bank rated 300Ah. As per the graph, if the DOD is 50 percent, it will last for about 3200 cycles. At 80 percent, the cycles reduce to 2100. So which of the two deliver more energy over the battery's life span? Let's do the math to figure it out.

To get the total energy delivered, multiply the battery bank's capacity by the DOD and by the number of cycles.

300 x (50/100) x 3200 = 480,000

300 x (80/100) x 2100 = 504,000

The lower DOD value gives the battery more cycles, but it ends up delivering less power.

The last two pointers to keep in mind are how much power you will use and the voltage you want the battery to operate at. Figuring this out will help you determine the configuration you will wire the batteries in. When buying batteries to create a battery bank, there are several nominal voltages to choose from. The most common are the 6V and the 12V. You can then take these batteries and connect them in a series-parallel configuration to get the voltage and capacities you want. If, for instance, you want your battery bank to have a voltage of 48V and a capacity of 300 Ah, then you will need to connect three 12V batteries to get 48V.

Step 3: Calculate the Number of Solar Panels You Will Need

Different sized modules will produce different amounts of power. When sizing your PV panel, you need to factor in things such as their power rating, your location, available sun hours, etc. However, the most important relationship you should be concerned with is the PV array's actual performance in relation to the battery bank. This is because the array is the primary power source and the main battery charger.

Your array needs to produce enough energy to satisfy your daily energy consumption; if it doesn't, the battery wouldn't recharge fully, and it will dip into the reserve supply meant to power the system during the days of autonomy. The amount of power you consume isn't a constant value; it changes throughout the year. For instance, you might use your lighting more during winter than in summer. This might lead you to design a system that caters for high consumption with a low power solar source. While this might work in winter, in summer, you will have an oversized system that will charge the battery bank fast and be underutilized the rest of the time. On top of that, the initial cost will be outrageous.

When sizing your array, you need to gather info on the site and make a few assumptions on the workings of the system. These values will help estimate the PV array you'll need to cover your energy consumption.

1. Take a look at the efficiency values of the system. To ensure the system produces enough power to cater to your needs, you must account for the energy losses. This means considering two main efficiency values: the battery's charging and discharging efficiency and the PV's energy delivery efficiency. For battery efficiency, a common value you can use is 85 percent; this value represents the internal energy losses and the charge controller's ability to charge the battery. The PV array's efficiency is affected by factors such as the array's temperature, how clean it is, voltage losses in the circuit, age of the array, etc. To get a true estimate of the PV's efficiency, you would have to individually calculate these losses and estimate their effect on the array. However, you can use an average value of 75 percent, and, although it's on the conservative side, it will help you get a steady power supply.

2. Factor in the total available solar resource
This is a combination of the shading effects, tilt effects, and the azimuth, which is the angle between North, measured clockwise around your horizon, and the sun. Figuring out the azimuth of your site tells you what direction to point your panel in. The total available solar resource is a percentage of how much energy your particular location can provide.

3. Settling on peak sun hours
Building a stand-alone system means that at some point, you will use an auxiliary power source such

as a generator. However, you want to reduce your overall reliance on such a device, if any at all. This means building a system based on the lowest amount of solar resource, which is in the middle of winter. Defining your peak hours during this time will allow you to continue to power your system when there's little to no sun.

Once you have defined all your variables:

- Gather the total energy values you calculated at the end of the load analysis. In our example, it was 760Wh (a combination of both AC and DC loads).
- Multiply the estimated PV and battery bank efficiencies; that is 75 percent x 85 percent = 64 percent. This will give you the estimated total efficiency of the array in charging the battery.
- Multiply this efficiency by the total available solar resource. In our case, it's 90 percent since about 10 percent is lost due to shading, the tilt angle, and the orientation of the sun. Our calculation will be 0.64 x 0.9 = 0.57.
- Now divide the total energy value by the result of the previous equation. Doing so will give you the daily amount of energy the PV array needs to produce. In this case its 760 / 0.57 = 1333.33 Wh.
- Lastly, divide this result by the amount of peak sun hours you decide to use. Suppose you have about 5 peak sun hours a day, then this means the array you build needs to produce 1333.33Wh in

5 hours. So, to get the size of the array in watts, divide 1333.33 by 5 = 266.7W. To power the system we are building, we need a PV array that produces 266. 7W. The actual performance of the system will vary depending on the season and irradiance levels.

Now that we know the array size, we can calculate how many modules we need. All you have to do is divide this figure by the standard power rating of the modules you want to use. For instance, if you use a 100W panel, you would need about 3 modules that is 266 / 100 = 2. 6 round this off to the nearest whole number to get 3. This means your system will be slightly oversized. Don't worry about it, though; you are better off building a system that produces too much power as opposed to not enough.

Step 4: Sizing Your Charge Controller

After sizing your battery bank and PV array, you need to figure out what size charge controller to use. There are two kinds of charge controllers, namely maximum power point tracking (MPPT) and pulse-width modulation (PWM) controllers. A PWM controller is set to match the input power of the battery regardless of the type of power generated by the panels. There is an inherent loss of power when using this controller. The MPPT, on the other hand, maximizes the optimal charging power of the PV at any given time. It allows the array to operate at its optimal power point regardless of the battery bank's voltage. The PWM cannot utilize this maximum charging point.

The charge controller you intend to use must be large enough to handle all the power produced by the system, which might mean you may end up using multiple controllers, especially if the array wattage exceeds what one charge controller can handle. Each controller might be connected to a different array, but all of them are connected to the same battery bank. When picking your charge controller, you need to factor in their voltage, power, and current specifications. Each controller has a voltage range that it must stay within. That is the maximum voltage it can accept and the minimum voltage it needs to stay above. Your job is to examine the temperature-adjusted voltages from the PV modules and match them to the charge controller's voltage range.

Once you know the temperature-adjusted voltages for the modules, you can use this figure to determine how many modules you need to wire in series for each string. All the module strings connected to the same charge controller must be the same length, and, unlike grid-tie inverters, they operate at lower voltages. This means using fewer modules such as 3 or 4 per string, whereas in grid-tie systems, you might find 8 to 10 modules per string. After figuring out how many modules you will connect in series, you need to determine the strings to connect in parallel based on your power requirements. Once you are done, finalize the controller specialization by factoring in the current requirements.

Once you determine the voltage window, you can pick a charge controller by looking at the relationship between the array's and the battery bank voltage. Most MPPTs can step down voltage, that is, take on higher voltages on the input side and reduce it on the battery side. Using such controllers gives you the freedom to create a system with more modules. If you used a controller without this feature, the voltage widow is smaller, and you are forced to use PV arrays and batteries with similar nominal voltages. Using a charge controller with a high voltage window reduces the number of wires running between the array and the controller. To deliver the same amount of power, a high voltage array needs to push less current through the conduit, and the amount of current flowing through them directly affects the conductor sizing.

This step-down feature also allows you to use modules with voltages that don't correspond to typical battery charging voltages. PWM controllers, on the flip side, need you to match the PV and battery bank voltages. This significantly reduces your voltage range, but it also means you don't have to go through the trouble of temperature-adjusting the module's voltage to that of the controller. The work's been done for you since the nominal voltage input must match the nominal voltage output. The drawback to this is you can't use any old module; you must use a module made for typical nominal battery voltages such as 12V or 24V and connect them in series as required. The main advantage of MPPTs over PWMs is you can almost use the full benefit of the power of the array, which equates to more efficient battery charging.

Aside from voltage specification, you also have to consider the power and current specifications when choosing your charge controller. You need to factor in these limitations to get a controller that's properly suited to your needs. Depending on the kind of controller you use, you have to examine the array's power and current levels. After making your power and current considerations, you might end up with a different sized array than before.

You want to pick a charger with a charge rate (C) of anywhere between C/10 and C/20. A high charge rate above C/10 will charge the battery too fast, meaning they won't charge efficiently, nor will they be able to take all the current being produced by the array. A low charge rate of below C/20 means it will take too long for the battery to fully charge. As per our example, we need a 248 Ah battery bank. You want the charging current from the array to land anywhere between 12 A and 24 A. That is 248 Ah divided by a charge rate of C/10 = 24 A or divided by a charge rate of C/20 = 12A. If the battery bank has a nominal voltage of 12V, then the PV array should be between 144W and 288W. This is still close to the figure we arrived at before: 266.7W.

Step 5: Sizing the Inverter

The next step is sizing the inverter. Just as with the controller, you need to consider the load voltages, maximum power drawn, its charging capabilities, especially from an AC source, and its ability to supply power when certain loads surge; that is, draw a lot of power in a short time.

Most inverters nowadays are inverter chargers which eliminate the hassle of designing a system with a separate inverter and charger.

The system you design might require using more than one inverter. You must ensure that they communicate with each other since different manufacturers have different specifications on this communication. Remember, with multiple inverters; the power output values are additive. For instance, if you have two 2 kW inverters, they can provide 4 kW of power to the loads.

Your energy consumption analysis helps determine the voltage needs of the appliances you will be using. For most residential equipment, this voltage is 120/240 VAC. However, most inverters come with a 120 VAC rating, meaning they have to be stacked to supply 240 VAC. An inverter's main job is delivering current and voltage to the loads; it's not concerned about energy consumption. This means that how long the loads run doesn't matter. That's why you should take extra care determining the inverter's power output needs using the energy consumption data you gathered in the beginning.

Inverters are always rated at their continuous power output value, so ensure the inverter you pick can provide the power you need. To do this, you need to estimate which loads will be running simultaneously, then add these values up to get the minimum power rating for the inverter. In our example, if every load is turned on, the total power drawn would be 760W, which is almost a kilowatt of power. If you think that there's even a slight chance that these loads will run simultaneously, you should get an inverter that's rated at a minimum AC output rating of 1 kW. If your system needs more power than one inverter can handle, consider stacking them. Also, factor in any future loads you might add to the system and get an inverter that suits those needs.

Inverters have the ability to deal with surges. These sudden power draws occur mostly with appliances that have motors such as water pumps, fridges, washing machines, etc. The surge occurs when it starts operating, and if the inverter cannot provide enough power for that brief period, the entire system might crash. Fortunately, inverters today can surge three to four times their rated output to start motors. To account for inevitable surges, you need to estimate how much power the inverter will provide and how much power will be drawn when the surge happens.

Adding these values will give you a rough estimate of how much power the inverter needs to produce to handle the surge. For instance, our system's inverter delivers about 1 kW of power to all the loads, but the fridge needs 0.8 kW to start. The inverter, therefore, needs to provide about 1.8 to 2 kW of power during the surge. This surge is specific to the appliance and is noted on the label as the maximum current draw. If it is not listed, you can use a clamp meter to register the power drawn when it starts or simply multiply the power rating of the appliance by 3.

Now that you are done with the math, you have a general idea of what your system will look like; Here's a wiring diagram to help you get a better mental picture of things.

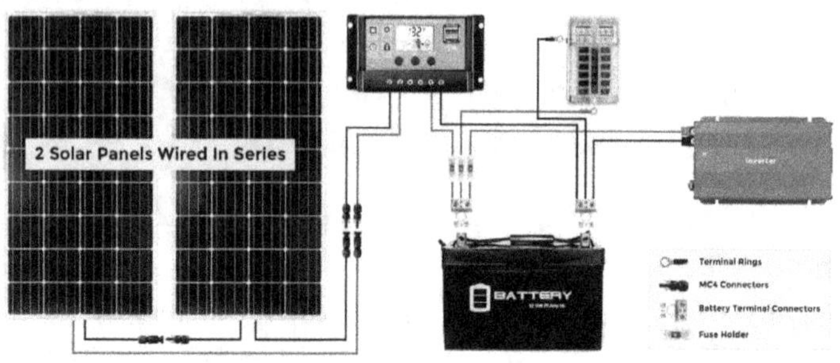

Step 6: Balancing the System

These are the final touches you need before you take off.

Wiring

Once you have identified all your components, the next step is figuring out the correct sizes for all the wires you will use. It's important to pay extra care when sizing your conduits; one missing piece could mean stopping everything. When sizing your conduits, you need to identify exactly where these wires will go because they have different requirements. For instance, wires running from the array to the inverter are different from those running out of the inverter to the distribution panel.

Defining circuits

A circuit is a path formed between the positive and negative terminals through which electrons run in to do useful work. For instance, the path followed by electrons from the modules through the inverter and back to the modules. Different conduits and wires are used to connect the various components in a PV system. The size and length of the wires needed and the safety devices used are determined by the circuit type and its location.

In a PV system, there are numerous circuits, such as the PV source circuit, which connects individual strings in the PV source circuit. These often run along the back of module strings leading to a junction box or a combiner box. From the junction box, wires can be combined to the DC disconnects, then to the inverter where it's converted to AC and transmitted to other loads. Conductors are defined by the roles they play in the various circuits, and, for both AC and DC circuits, they should be grounded.

Most wires are made from copper because it's a good conductor, and it's compatible with terminations, areas where conductors are attached to disconnects, inverters, circuit breakers, etc. There are also aluminum conductors, but aluminum is viewed as an inferior wiring material because it's less conductive than copper. When picking what wire to use, here are a few pointers to keep in mind.

Wires are always designated by an acronym that describes the wire's properties. For instance, USE stands for underground service entrance wire.

- Most wires will have multiple acronyms listed on them. As long as one of the properties listed meets your requirements, you can use the wire.

- PV modules come with two copper wires prein-stalled with quick connect plugs to help make things easier during installation. These are often USE cables that connect the module directly to the inverter. Because these wires are installed on the back of the PV module, they are subject to harsh weather conditions such as full sunlight and high temperatures. Luckily they are sunlight, heat, and moisture resistant. They can be found in various sizes and colors, which can help make finding the one you need easier. Don't run these cables inside buildings because they are not fire-retardant and are not suited for indoor locations; for this, you need to use indoor wiring.

PV wire is a cross-linked copper wire that uses poly-ethylene for insulation that was developed from a need for a conductor that can be used with a transformer-le inverter. The two layers of polyethylene offer more pro-tection than the single insulated USE cables. This wire is used inside PV source circuits that connect the individual PV strings to the junction or combiner box.

To draw power from the junction box to the rest of the system, you can use standard building wiring such as heat-resistance thermoplastic or moisture resistance ther-moplastic. This relatively cheap wiring can be used for both DC and AC circuits, but you need to ensure you protect the wiring from moisture, heat, and physical dam-age by running them through conduits. I recommend us-ing the moisture-resistant thermoplastic wire because it has an additional temperature rating. Since the cables will be running outside, they are exposed to extreme temperatures, and this type of wire works well in such conditions.

For the battery, you want cabling that is moisture and heat resistant. But any wire can work; just ensure that it is properly rated and the connectors you use are also properly rated, or else they might fail, putting the system and your safety at risk. All wiring used in the battery is in a corrosive environment, and so you must ensure that the wire you go for is designated for use in such conditions.

Grounding Your Electrics

Working with a solar-powered system carries with it some risks such as dealing with the direct current from the array, high currents flowing to the battery bank, and the AC coming from the inverter. Except for very small systems such as lighting, all PV systems should be grounded. This means all exposed metal parts should be connected to a ground; that is, the rack, frames, metal boxes, etc. This means running a wire from a negative terminal into an earthing rod. This grounding ensures the safety of the system in case of a fault in the system. In battery-based systems, it's recommended to connect one of the current-carrying conductors that's close to the battery to the ground as batteries are the second-largest source of power in the system next to the array.

These grounding connections prevent the buildup of static electricity and prevent you from getting affected by the high voltages running in the circuit in case of a fault. When installing the array, you must include the grounding connection from the array itself since it is a large power source. If you are using both AC and DC electronics in your system, they require different grounds. If you are electrocuted by AC, even though the shock might be fatal, you are likely to get thrown back and let go of whatever is shocking you. With DC, there's a constant flow of charge going through you, meaning you can't let go of whatever is shocking you. This means that even low levels of DC are dangerous, with high DC current likely to cause more fatal injuries than a similar amount of AC.

The thing with DC is you are unlikely to notice any jolt of current even if you short-circuit the system with your fingers. And since PV panels still produce a small amount of electricity even at night, it poses a big safety risk. The solution is using isolation circuit breakers and a good ground that will switch the system off in case of a fault. With AC, you also need to install these isolation switches between the inverter and the distribution panel to isolate the PV array.

In instances where you are installing the PV system on a boat or an RV, you cannot connect the earthing rod to the ground. If your system is powered by a 100 W PV array, you might only need one ground for all your components. In a larger system that produces more current, a grounding plane is used. This is a high-capacity cable running from the battery's negative end to the other components that need to be grounded. Alternatively, you can use a metal frame such as the RV body as the ground for your system.

Circuit Protection

Disconnects

For both safety and maintenance reasons, you need to install a way for the conductors to disconnect themselves from all power sources in case of a fault. The exact location of these disconnects will depend on the system, but the function is the same. There are different ways to integrate disconnects into your system; for instance, you cause an inverter with a disconnect integrated into it. These can disconnect the DC circuit from the inverter and the AC circuit at the same time.

They are an easy way to meet code requirements, but there are cases where you will need visible disconnects. The second type of disconnects are positioned outside the inverter and individually connected to a single circuit. That is one for the DC side and another for the AC side. This way, you can get to both circuits safely. Disconnects can serve as a form of overcurrent protection, much like a circuit breaker.

Overcurrent Protection Devices

The wires used in your PV system need protection from the possibility of too much current flowing through them. If this happens, the overcurrent protection devices such as fuses and circuit breakers prevent too much current from going through the wires until you manually reset the system.

- Circuit breakers - they are often installed in the main distribution panel and are very similar to those found in your house. If too much current flows through them, the breaker trips, breaking the circuit, which stops the current in its tracks. They are often installed on the AC side of things but can be installed on the DC side for low voltage systems. Don't use them on the DC side of high voltage systems because they are not properly rated for this use and might fail. Most of these breakers are thermally activated, tripping when they reach a certain temperature. What's great about circuit breakers is when they trip, you just reset them; you don't need to replace them. Circuit breakers are made for specific uses, so you have to get a breaker manufactured for the exact panel you are using. However, since we are custom making our system, you are better off using those calibrated for specific current and voltage ratings.
- Fuses – when dealing with high voltage DC circuits or when you need an overcurrent protection device placed outside a load center, you install a fuse. These devices work similarly to circuit breakers, except you have to replace them once they 'trip.' A fuse contains a small filament wire in a case that remains intact as long as it doesn't get

too hot. If too much current flows, the wire heats up and melts, interrupting the circuit. Similar to circuit breakers, they have ratings that indicate in what systems they can be used. Even though they have both AC and DC ratings, the voltages vary, meaning you have to ensure the fuse you use has the correct rating. Fuses provide both overcurrent protection and a means of disconnecting the circuit.

Final Words

After installing the PV system, you need to check and see if everything is working as it should. This is known as commissioning the system, but before you get too excited and start turning everything on, you need to ensure everything is correctly installed. Conducting these preliminary checks ensures your system is safe and won't damage your equipment. Photovoltaic systems are ideally low maintenance, not no-maintenance. This means you still have to check on the system once in a while to ensure everything is doing what it's supposed to.

Here's a simple maintenance schedule you can follow

As required:

Try and clean the PV array to remove any dust, grime, snow, leaves, etc. If you can easily access your panels, using a dirt and rain repellent glass polish can help keep your panel cleaner for longer.

Monthly:

Check the performance of your solar array. You want to ensure that it's performing as per your expectations depending on the time of year. You can even log the performance and compare it from year to year. This monthly check will help you easily identify any issues in case there's a drop in performance.

Every three months:

You can check on the battery bank and its storage area. Ensure it's still well-ventilated, and there's enough electrolyte. Check there are no leaks, and it is still weatherproof. Clean any visible dirt off the battery. Perform a visual check of the connectors and wiring.

Yearly:

Swap out the order of the batteries in your battery bank; place the batteries that were in the middle on either end to help even out the wear.

Make a list and check everything off as you go. This way you won't miss anything. For instance, you can decide to start with the mechanical elements and check if the mounting is secure? Was the correct hardware used to install the footings? Are the modules properly grounded? Is the rack properly attached to the mounting system? And more. Next, repeat this process but with the electrical elements. For instance, did you install enough modules? Are they properly connected? What about the batteries? Are they properly installed? Are they properly vented? Are the charge controller and inverter correctly installed? What about the disconnects and overcharge protection devices? Did you use the proper wire gauges to connect the array to the inverter? Etc.

Safety is a vital aspect when working with PV systems; this means that you must put your safety and that of the system at the forefront at every level. For instance, when working on PV systems, you must wear proper protective gear and never work on live circuits, etc.

Thanks to advancements in solar technology, you might have even more advanced solar cell technologies readily available to you, meaning your system might not be as huge but can still provide as much power. Right now, most cells have an efficiency of 15 to 20 percent, meaning about 80 to 85 percent of the sun's solar energy goes unused. Watch out for these and other emerging technologies so you can upgrade wherever necessary.

This book provides you with the methodology of how to design an off-grid solar power system. In the first chapter, we went through the basics of solar electricity, looked at where solar energy comes from, and delved into a bit of its history. The second chapter covered the steps to follow when determining your needs and thus your budget. This involves everything from thinking about the scope of the project to calculating how much energy you need, selecting the right components, and even creating a detailed design of the system. The third and fourth chapters covered some of the electrical knowledge you need to be familiar with and the common components in a solar-powered system. In the last chapter, we put everything together and detailed how to properly size your system. With this information, you can confidently design and build a system of any capacity.

Living off-grid is an inspiration to many people; however, be under no illusions: you will need to make some changes and compromises to make your off-grid dream come true. Living in your RV, camper, or boat might be a once-in-a-while thing, and the energy usage is different if you lived there every day. If you plan on living off-grid all the time, you need to make several lifestyle changes to make it all work. Hopefully, you are inspired to design and build your own off-grid PV system.

Image Credit: Shutterstock.com

www.ingramcontent.com/pod-product-compliance
Lightning Source LLC
Chambersburg PA
CBHW071928120726
48001CB00005B/1918